TABLE OF C

MW01027316

INTRODUCTION

"What do the doctors know?"

That's one of those questions that are universal to all cultures and times. And until a century or two ago, the answer would have been a resounding, "Not a hell of a lot!"

Most medical knowledge that has vanquished diseases and conditions once considered incurable has come to us fairly recently—far more recently, in fact, than advances in the arts, industry, and other sciences.

Michelangelo sculpted the statue of David and Shakespeare wrote *Hamlet* long before doctors knew that the heart pumps blood through the body. The industrial revolution was transforming life in America and Europe before doctors realized that germs caused diseases and that it was important for hospitals to be clean.

Nowadays, any second grader would be insulted if you implied that he or she didn't know these things. But until recently, the best physicians did not.

In the absence of knowledge, theories of all description about dis-

6

eases and their cures abounded; often the absurd appeared rational. Included in this book are some of the more outlandish practices that were once accepted by physicians as valid cures. A few, it seems, were thought up out of the blue; others were more understandable misreadings of the facts as they were known. Some were downright quackery, but most  were advocated by honorable men doing the best they could with the knowledge they had. Some "cures" were benign in their ineffectiveness; others were positively lethal.

Understandably, people mistrusted doctors. "There is no quicker way to health than to do without a doctor," said Petrarch in the fourteenth century; he ordered his servants to keep doctors away should he fall ill. Joseph Addison in 1711 observed, "When a nation abounds in physicians it grows thin of people." And even in the 1800s Oliver

Wendell Holmes Sr., a professor of medicine at Harvard, wrote, "If all the medicine in the world were thrown into the sea, it would be bad for the fish and good for humanity."

To us moderns, many of the old cures aren't as threatening as they are silly. Then again, we're lucky enough to have been born after Pasteur, Lister, Salk, and others who have made our ailments more bearable and survivable. Perhaps, after another century or two of medical progress, some of our present-day cures will look weird, too.

CURE-ALLS

LINCOLN'S BLUE PERIOD

What's wrong with this list?

1. TEETHING POWDER

2. LAXATIVES

3. DE-WORMER

4. TUNA FISH SANDWICH

5. DISINFECTANT

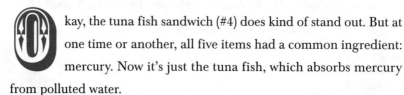

kay, the tuna fish sandwich (#4) does kind of stand out. But at one time or another, all five items had a common ingredient: mercury. Now it's just the tuna fish, which absorbs mercury from polluted water.

Today mercury is widely recognized as a highly toxic chemical, attacking the nervous system. It's been linked to personality changes including anxiety, hostility, depression, insomnia, and memory loss. It also causes some grotesque physical results, such as ulcerated gums, dis-

colored teeth, rashes, and liver and kidney damage.

But for more than 2,000 years, mercury was considered a cure-all. Physicians to the first emperor of China gave him mercury pills to help him in his bid for immortality. (Instead he died, cutting short the Qin dynasty after only 15 years.) In the nineteenth century, it was prescribed for ailments including apoplexy (stroke or hemorrhage), tuberculosis, toothache, and constipation.

It was dispensed as a little blue pill, known as "blue mass." In addition to mercury, the pill contained licorice root, rosewater, honey, sugar, and rose petals. If taken at the normally prescribed dose of the time—one pill two or three times a day—it would deliver nearly 9,000 times the amount of mercury that is deemed safe by current health standards.

Among the people taking mercury pills was a future president of the United States, Abraham Lincoln, according to a study published in 2001 in *Perspectives in Biology and Medicine*. Apparently it was prescribed for melancholy, or depression, a disorder that plagued Lincoln throughout his life. But it didn't do much good. In fact, his moods became positively, well, mercurial.

Here I am after a course of MERCURY, my teeth and gums rather the worse for it; my hair all gone, and my breath having become most intolerably offensive.

"There seem to be clear, qualitative changes in his underlying behavior during the 1850s," says Norbert Hirschhorn, a medical historian and the lead author of the study. "The gloom becomes impenetrable. He becomes subject to towering rages and outbursts of bizarre behavior—jumping up suddenly and running out of the house for no reason, bursts of inappropriate laughter."

The authors of the study cited numerous accounts of friends and fellow lawyers who traveled the legal circuit with the man who was destined to lead our country through its greatest domestic crisis. One contemporary described Lincoln's face in anger as "lurid with majestic and terrifying wrath." Another described him as "so angry that he looked like Lucifer in an uncontrollable rage."

During an 1858 debate with Stephen Douglas, his rival for a seat in the U.S. Senate, Lincoln became so enraged that he grabbed a former aide and shook him until his teeth chattered.

"Mercury poisoning certainly could explain Lincoln's known neurological symptoms: insomnia, tremor, and the rage attacks," said Robert G. Feldman, a professor at Boston University's School of

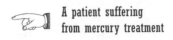
A patient suffering
from mercury treatment

Medicine and Public Health and a co-author of the report.

Luckily, a few months after he was inaugurated as President in 1861, Lincoln told his good friend John T. Stuart that he had quit taking the little blue pills because they made him "cross."

It was none too soon. Lincoln's decision to go cold turkey had extremely important consequences. "Faced with as great stresses as any President, Lincoln demonstrated incredible maturity, calm, and steadiness at the helm," Hirschhorn said. "He might not have had that capacity if he had continued taking blue mass. That insight may have been crucial to the outcome of the Civil War."

Who ordered the tuna fish?

SMOKE SCREEN

ot even the most militant American smoker nowadays would say tobacco is good for you. But from the time Europeans discovered the weed growing in the New World, many believed it had medicinal properties. Smoking reputedly strengthened the stomach, served as a gentle laxative, and stopped inflammation of nose and throat membranes. Doctors recommended smoking  and snuff-taking to calm the insane. Green leaves were said to salve gunshot wounds, heal cuts and bruises, cleanse ulcers, and even cure leprosy.

Health claims didn't stop with folk medicine. Tobacco companies advertised benefits of their product well into the twentieth century, until the Federal Trade Commission cracked down on their unsubstantiated—and ridiculous—assertions.

Camel cigarettes, the ads said, aid digestion "no matter where, what or when one eats, at odd hours and in all sorts of places." A Camel

"picks up, perks up, renews and restores bodily energy," the ads further claimed; it also relieves fatigue and gives athletes a competitive edge.

Kool cigarettes were said to prevent the common cold.

Kent's "Micronite" filter offered the "greatest health protection in cigarette history," P. Lorillard claimed in 1952. Its health-giving ingredient? That substance widely associated with cancer: asbestos! (Lorillard discontinued the Micronite filter in 1956.)

L&M cigarettes advertised that its "alpha cellulose" filter was "just what the doctor ordered." Hopefully, that doctor had his license revoked.

Thanks to medical research—and not a little common sense—any residual belief in the U.S. that smoking was healthy finally went up in smoke.

But in China things are different. The website of the government-run tobacco monopoly claims that cigarettes are an excellent way to prevent ulcers, reduce the risk of Parkinson's disease, relieve schizophrenia, boost brain cells, improve reactions, increase efficiency, and prevent loneliness and depression. In other words, they do everything but shine your shoes.

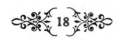

No medical evidence is cited, nor is any mention made of—what's that disease?—lung cancer.

China is the world's largest tobacco market, with 360 million smokers, and 3 million added each year. An estimated 1,300,000 Chinese smokers die annually but, hey, they seem to be saying that the health benefits are to die for.

SICK? GO TO YOUR MUMMY

From ancient times until the 1700s, powdered mummies were thought to have medicinal qualities that healed wounds and cured such conditions as epilepsy and vertigo. But in those pre-FDA days, the buyer needed to be wary of inferior mummies.

French medical writer Pierre Pomet, in his 1691 *History of Drugs*, advised readers to avoid unscrupulous mummy dealers. In parts of Africa, he wrote, they would sell "white mummies" which were made by burying drowned travelers in the desert sand. Pomet advised his readers to insist on a mummy "of a good shining Black, not full of bones or dirt, of a good smell, and which being burnt does not stink of pitch."

He made no mention of checking the expiration date.

ALL IN VEIN

F or many centuries, medical treatment was based on the belief that there were four bodily "humors:" blood, phlegm, yellow bile, and black bile. Disease, it was thought, was caused by an imbalance in these humors, and good health was restored by purging, starving, vomiting, or bloodletting to recover the balance.

Bloodletting was a common cure-all from ancient times until well into the nineteenth century. In the Middle Ages it was performed by barbers, which explains their traditional pole. The red is for blood, the white represents the tourniquet, and the pole itself is for the stick the patient squeezed to dilate his veins.

Typically one to four pints of blood were drained, until the patient became faint. Cuts were often made in several different areas of the body, and blood was gathered in a shallow bowl.

The practice came to America on the *Mayflower*. A strong advocate in eighteenth-century America was Dr. Benjamin Rush, a signer of the Declaration of Independence, who is admired for his intelligence and civic

Breathing a vein.

commitment, particularly by those willing to ignore his bizarre medical theories. He treated George Washington for acute laryngitis by draining nine pints of blood in 24 hours; Washington died soon afterward.

In 1861, Mrs. Isabella Beeton strongly advised in her popular *Book of Household Management* that the patient should always be bled while standing or sitting up—never lying down. It's hard to argue with her logic:

> "If, as is often the case, [the patient] should happen to faint, he can, in most cases at least, easily be brought to again by the operator placing him flat on his back and stopping the bleeding." If the patient is bled while lying down, however, "what could be done to bring him to again?" The "operator" cannot make the patient lie down since he's "in that position already, and cannot be placed lower than it at present is . . . except, as is most likely the case, under the ground."

For the devices used to draw blood, see page 49.

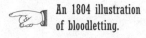

An 1804 illustration of bloodletting.

BOTANICAL CURES

LOOKS ARE EVERYTHING

Finding a cure for a disease isn't as mysterious as it may seem, according to the Doctrine of Signatures. Just look for something in nature that reminds you of your problem and you're halfway to curing it.

- Have a bad headache? Try nutmeg, which resembles a brain. Or a poppy, whose fruit resembles a human head.
- Something wrong with your blood? Look to red roses, of course.
- Toothache? Try henbane, whose seed container is shaped like a jaw.

Belief in such cures originated in Egypt or Babylonia and appeared in European medical books straight through the seventeenth century. After that, the medical establishment realized that any resemblance between the shapes of body parts and the shapes of the cures was purely coincidental, and doctors no longer signed off on the Doctrine of Signatures.

SUFFERING FROM NOSEBLEEDS? HERE'S A SIMPLE CURE

English druggists in the seventeenth century sold the greenish moss that is found in the heads and skulls of the dead. To be effective the moss, called usnea, had to be from the skull of a man who had died violently and was then exposed to the elements. The source was often Ireland, where hanged criminals were customarily left on the gallows until they fell to pieces. Usnea was reported to be effective for treating, among other conditions, nervous disorders and nosebleeds.

DOWN WITH DOCTORS!

The United States was founded by those who denounced authority, so it should be no surprise that doctors would find many detractors in the young country. The best known was Samuel A. Thomson (1769–1843), who had little use for disease theory and traditional medications. All ills, he said, were produced by cold, and any treatment that produced heat would help cure them.

He developed seventy plant remedies, some of which caused vomiting and heavy sweating, and spread the word through his Botanico-Medical College of Ohio and his Friendly Botanic Societies in New England. His disciples, called Thomsonians, staged annual conventions

that resembled revival meetings.

The Thomsonians' success inspired imitators, who called themselves Neo-C, Eclectics, and Reformed Practitioners of Medicine. All shared a belief in natural healing and a distaste for what they considered the mercenary and pernicious practices of conventional physicians.

Thomsonian therapy probably didn't cure anyone. But if it didn't kill anyone, it may have been ahead of conventional medicine at the time.

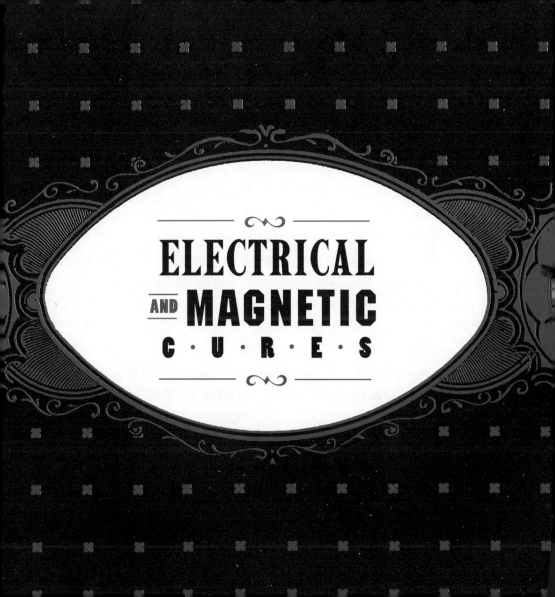

THE BODY ELECTRIC

From MRIs to nerve stimulation, electricity has been a boon to modern medicine. And to think, it all began with a fish.

Because some fish—including, of course, electric eels—can deliver a powerful jolt, fishermen had been using them since early times to numb pain. Then Scribonius, a Roman physician, recommended placing a live torpedo fish underfoot to treat gout. "The patient must stand on a moist shore washed by the sea and he should stay like this until his whole foot and leg up to the knee is numb," he wrote in the first century B.C.

Doctors also prescribed electric fish for headache, epilepsy, joint pain, depression, and a condition called *prolapsus ani*, in which the rectum protrudes through the anus—though they didn't say where to place *that* fish.

HOT TUBS

I f there were a *People* magazine in eighteenth-century Europe, the doctor likeliest to make the cover would undoubtedly have been Franz Mesmer—a purple-robed Austrian whose miraculous cures were all the rage in Vienna and Paris.

According to Mesmer, everything that acted on the body—gravity, magnetism, electricity, heat, and light—was mediated by a "universal fluid." People got sick wherever too much or too little of the fluid collected; they were cured with the application of magnets to restore the proper flow. Eventually Mesmer dispensed with magnets, merely pointing an iron wand at the patient, or even passing his hands over the afflicted area. People convulsed violently—though sometimes they slept or danced; then they pronounced themselves cured.

In the court of King Louis XVI, Mesmer developed the first group therapy. He would seat a number of patients holding hands around a *bacquet*, a wooden tub full of glass powder and iron filings. Bottles filled with "magnetic" water protruded from the tub's top, with metal rods inside to

aim magnetic rays at the sitters. Soothing music filtered out from behind curtains covered with astrological symbols. Then Mesmer, in his long purple robe, would enter and touch the afflicted with a white wand.

Steven Spielberg couldn't have made it more captivating. As science, however, it left a lot to be desired. In 1784 the dubious French king appointed a commission to investigate the charismatic doctor; its chairman was our own Benjamin Franklin, ambassador from the newly established United States. The group reported that Mesmer's cures were due largely to "imagination and to imitation"—in other words, it's all in your head.

Discredited, Mesmer left Paris. He died in Switzerland at the ripe old age of 85, leaving nothing to the progress of medicine but somewhat enriching our language. Today, the word *mesmerizing* is widely used to mean hypnotizing or spellbinding.

Franz Mesmer introduces his patients to his "bacquet"—a wooden tub filled with glass powders and iron filings.

SOWING GREENBACKS

Illness provides fertile ground for bizarre cures. And that was the field plowed profitably by Elisha Perkins and his "tractors."

A Connecticut doctor with a sideline in mule trading, Perkins believed that metals could draw disease out of the body. In 1795 he patented the Perkins "metallic tractor," a pair of rods, each three inches long and tapering to a point. One rod was supposed to be an alloy of copper, zinc, and gold, the other an alloy of iron, silver, and platinum—although, in reality, they were only brass and steel.

Stroked across the afflicted surface of the body for 20 minutes at a time, Perkins said, the tractors would draw off "the noxious electrical fluid that lay at the root of the suffering." The tractors could relieve "pains in the head, face, teeth, breast, side, stomach, back, rheumatism, and some gouts."

Perkins boasted he'd cured 5,000 people, and he sold his tractors—at a hefty $25 for a pair of rods—by the thousands. Customers included ministers, physicians, congressmen, the Chief Justice of the Supreme Court, and George Washington himself.

Most of the medical establishment was skeptical, however, and in 1796 the Connecticut Medical Society, which Perkins had co-founded, kicked him out. Three years later, when New York was ravaged by yellow fever, Perkins arrived with his tractors to save lives and restore his own reputation.

The tractors plowed barren ground. Perkins caught the fever himself and died.

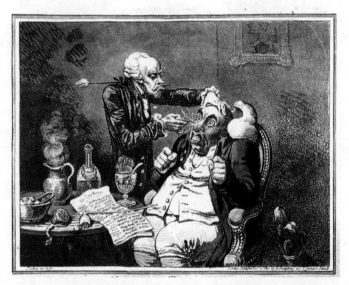

In this 1801 illustration, a doctor applies metallic tractors to a patient, igniting his nose and knocking off his wig.

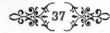

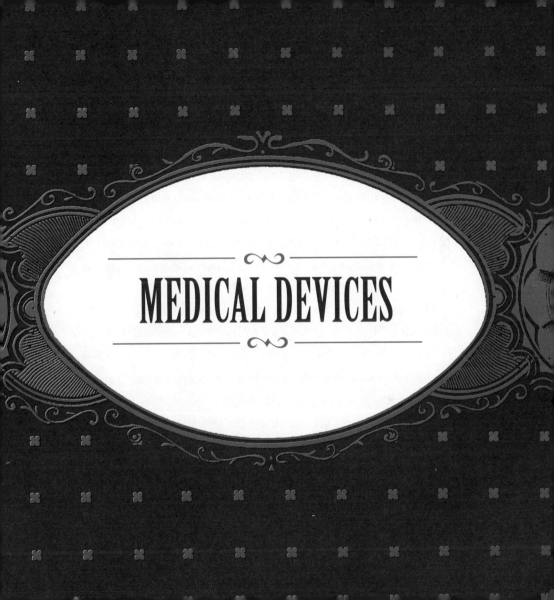

MEDICAL DEVICES

HARD TO SWALLOW

oin' fishin'" is an activity you might expect of a doctor on his day off. But for Alpheus Myers, a doctor in Logansport, Indiana, in the 1800s, it was all in a day's work.

In his rural practice, Myers must have seen so many patients with tapeworms that he was struck by the spirit of invention. And so in 1854 he procured a patent for a "new and useful Trap for Removing Tapeworms from the Stomach and Intestines."

The Trap, as described in the patent, consisted of a spring-loaded cylinder of gold, platinum, or other rustproof metal, about three-quarters of an inch long and one-quarter of an inch in diameter, attached to a cord. An interior cylinder held the bait, which may be "any nutritious substance." (Dr. Myers suggested cheese.)

Before the trap could be deployed the patient had to fast for up to a week. This guaranteed that the worm would be hungry enough to "ascend into the stomach, and even sometimes into the throat." The patient was to swallow the trap and, with the cord dangling from his

mouth, he was "left to his ease from about six to twelve hours." Dr. Myers predicted that during this time the unsuspecting worm would seize the bait and the trap would close. The spring must be only strong enough to hold the worm and not strong enough to cut its head off, Dr. Myers cautioned.

How can you tell there's been a bite? Either the patient will sense it, or there will be a tug on the cord. "The patient should rest for a few hours after the capture, and then by gentle pulling at the cord the trap and worm will with ease and perfect safety be withdrawn."

If 12 hours pass without a nibble, the patent notes, it's time to pull up the trap, rebait it, and swallow again.

Evidently it worked—at least once. A year after his trap was patented, *Scientific American* reported that Dr. Myers had used the trap to remove a worm "50 feet in length, from a patient, who, since then, has had a new lease on life."

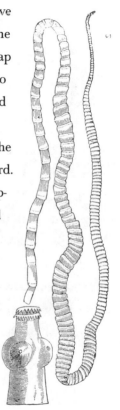

RAYS OF HOPE

I t could cure cancer. It could win wars. Surely a little radiation would be good for a youngster's enlarged tonsils?

Touted as a cure for everything from hay fever to old age, radium and radiation were all the rage in the first half of the twentieth century. Some doctors gave injections of radium and applied it topically in creams. When World War I kept Americans away from the spas of Europe, the U.S. Surgeon General said they'd do just as nicely drinking or dunking in tap water charged with radium. Soon devices like the Revigator, a crock lined with radioactive ore that emitted radon gas, were selling briskly.

If radioactive water were therapeutic, wouldn't X-rays be beneficial, too? Doctors routinely used high-dose X-rays on children to shrink enlarged tonsils, adenoids, and thymus glands. Dermatologists liked it for acne, birthmarks, and fungal infections of the scalp. Not to be left behind, shoe stores invited customers to stick their feet into fluoroscopes to test the fit of a new pair of shoes.

As it turned out, radiation wasn't the best medicine. Children whose scalps were irradiated lost their hair. Eventually some of the people whose necks were X-rayed developed thyroid nodules—abnormal growths or lumps in the thyroid gland. So kids who had hoped to avoid tonsillectomies sometimes underwent surgery to have the nodules removed instead.

The thirst for radium water devices subsided in the 1930s when a prominent patient died. By the mid-1960s, the medical establishment had mostly given up frivolous X-raying. The shoe stores had, too. And soon radon was perceived as such a threat that homes were routinely equipped with meters to detect the gas.

A flouroscope, used to test the fit of shoes.

THE UNKINDEST CUT

arious instruments were used to puncture veins and draw off blood—all of them less merciful than today's hypodermic needles. For more on bloodletting, see page 23.

* **LANCETS** sliced into veins to get the blood flowing; a spring-loaded version, popular in the eighteenth and nineteenth centuries, fired a blade into the vein. Oliver Wendell Holmes, a prominent nineteenth-century physician, described lancets as "the magician's wand of the dark ages of medicine."

* **FLEAMS** had several shafts that folded up like a pocketknife, each with a different-sized cutting blade.

* **SCARIFICATORS** looked especially cruel. Each had a set of 12 spring-driven rotary blades. Released by trigger, the blades made several quick, shallow cuts.

* **GLASS CUPS** were sometimes used after the skin was cut. Alcohol was burned in the cup to create a vacuum. Once the flame burned out, the cup was applied to a wound to speed up bleeding.

* Last, but not least repulsive: LEECHES. Calling somebody a leech is no compliment today, but for centuries the little bloodsuckers were a mainstay of medicine. The very word "leech" is from the Anglo-Saxon word *loece*, to heal. (Medieval doctors proudly called themselves leeches, a term applied more often nowadays to lawyers.)

A leech is typically two to four inches long; with a good liquid meal, it can expand to seven times its normal size. Leeches were used to draw blood in places too awkward for other bloodletting instruments, such as the gums, lips, nose, and fingers or even "the mouth of the womb," according to a 1634 medical text. In the nineteenth century, leeches were prescribed for everything from colds to obesity. They were so popular that they became an endangered species in Europe.

When it became clear in the nineteenth century that disease was caused by microorganisms rather than an imbalance of humors, bloodletting fell out of favor. So did the use of leeches—though they were still used occasionally when doctors ran out of other ideas. James Joyce was leeched around one eye in 1922 in a futile effort to halt his advancing blindness. Leeches were also used in a last-ditch effort to keep Joseph Stalin alive in 1953. Perhaps his doctors thought that one bloodsucker could help another.

Bloodletting is unlikely to make a comeback, but leeches are enjoying a revival (see page 130).

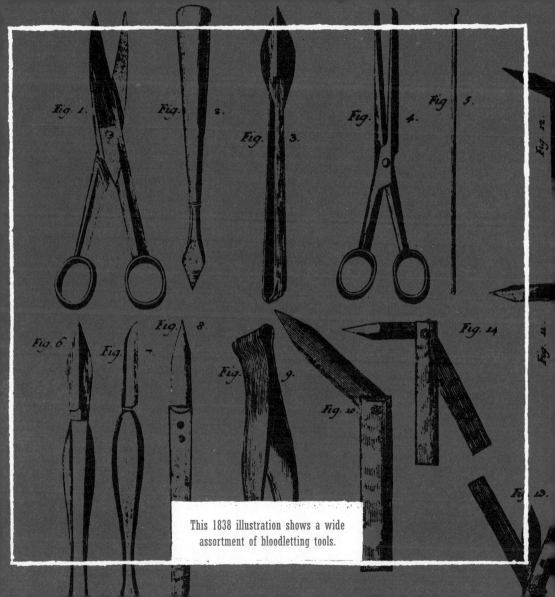

This 1838 illustration shows a wide assortment of bloodletting tools.

LIMITED VISION

Georg Bartisch (1535–1606) is known as the "Father of Modern Opthalmology." He wrote one of the first books on the subject and was hailed as a skilled eye surgeon who pioneered such procedures as cataract operations. But there was a cure he *didn't* prescribe: eyeglasses. He simply couldn't imagine that an eye that doesn't see well could do better with something in front of it.

A man reads a book written by Georg Bartisch.

A sixteenth-century illustration of Georg Bartisch's surgical procedure for cataracts.

SURGICAL AND POST-OP CURES

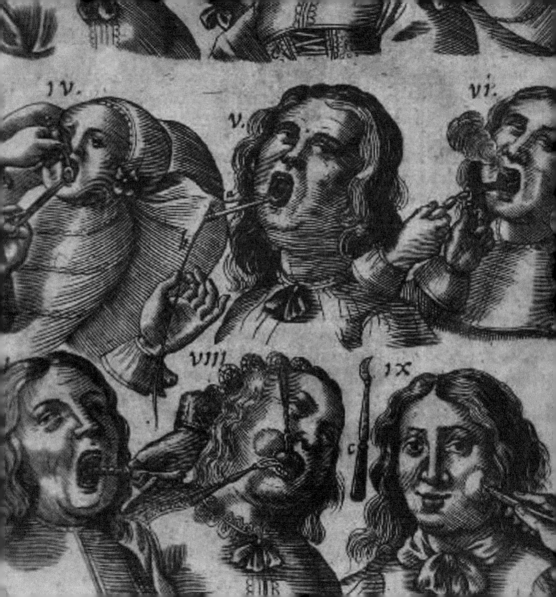

B-B-BITE YOUR TONGUE

Surgery can fix a cleft palate, so shouldn't it correct a stutter? That was the notion, anyway, of Johann Friedrich Dieffenbach, a surgeon in Berlin in the 1800s. "The idea lately suggested itself to me," he wrote, "that an incision carried completely through the root of the tongue might be useful in stuttering, which had resisted other means of cure."

Dieffenbach's operation consisted of slicing into the tongue and excising a triangular wedge. (Later surgeons would also remove the adenoids and, for good measure, drill into the skull to stop speech defects.)

One of Dieffenbach's first patients was a 13-year-old boy who, it is reported, "stuttered in Latin and French as well as in his own language." After the surgery, the boy reportedly remarked, "There is some blood running down my shirt." It was not recorded whether he said it in German, Latin, or French—or whether he stuttered.

A seventeenth-century illustration of palate and tongue surgery.

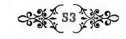

GOT PUS?

Most of us know that pus indicates bacterial infection. But to physicians from ancient Greece to the late nineteenth century, the right kind of pus—known as "laudable pus"—was often considered essential for healing wounds.

At a time when most surgical wounds became infected, infections could be classified into two categories: those with pus, and those without. Physicians observed that wounds that produced a creamy yellow ooze tended to take months to heal, but more of these patients survived than those whose wounds had a thin, watery discharge.

It was a logical next step to conclude that pus was good for you. Accordingly, doctors began deliberately inducing infections and fevers. No pus? Get "wool as greasy as can be procured, dip it in very little water, add one third wine, boil to good consistency," and insert in the wound, one early tract advised.

By the mid-nineteenth century, it was widely accepted that leaving an infection in an incision after a cancer operation could actually

benefit the patient. Even gangrene—the death of body tissues sometimes caused by infection—had its advocates. Stanislas Tanchou, a
Parisian cancer "expert," sagely observed, "It is remarkable that . . . gangrene [has] caused the largest number of cures. Gangrene may be
considered as a therapeutic agent, whether it occurs spontaneously or
is induced medically."

Actually, gangrene may be considered a lead-up to amputation.
Nothing laudable about that.

YOU MIGHT THINK YOU NEED THIS LIKE YOU NEED A HOLE IN YOUR HEAD...

o you think that evil spirits are making you sick? Or are you just fed up with headaches? Maybe you should consider having a hole cut in your skull.

This practice is called trepanation, the same term used in brain surgery to describe cutting into the skull. It is the oldest surgical practice known, dating from the Stone Age, and is still practiced by some tribes in Africa—and by at least a few people in America and England.

The theory was that cutting a small hole in a person's skull would relieve the soul from some devil or evil spirit that was tormenting it, or would relieve pressure on the brain. Clearly, the operation required a steady hand.

In modern times, a non-practicing doctor named Bart Hughes performed the operation on himself using an electric drill and a scalpel in order to achieve higher consciousness. One of his followers is an Englishwoman named Amanda Fielding, who ran for Parliament on a

platform that called for free trepanation from the National Health Service. She received 40 votes. She claims that her own trepanning has given her more energy, inspiration, and a "permanent natural high." She also claims that the trepanned are "better prepared to fight neuroses and depression and less likely to become prone to alcoholism and drug addiction."

Nobody would say she's not open-minded.

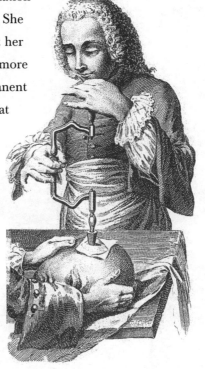

A physician applies trepanation to a boy's skull. Trepanation is the oldest surgical practice known, dating from the Stone Age.

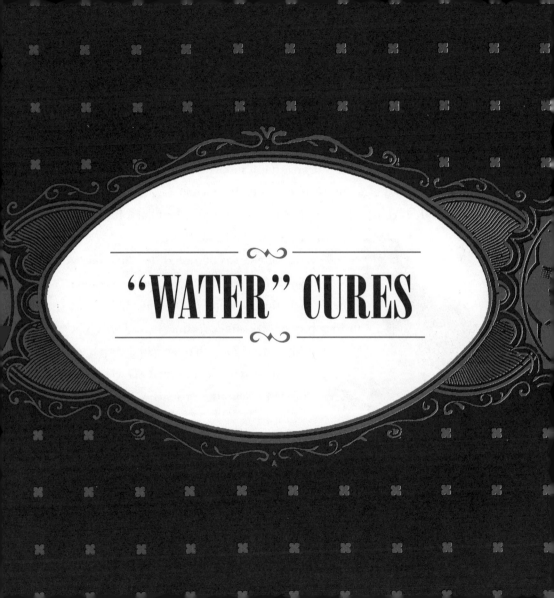

"WATER" CURES

HERE'S WATER IN YOUR GUT

ncient Egyptians were afraid of stuff rotting in their guts and bowels, and put great faith in enemas, believing that they had been invented by a god, ibis-headed Thoth. Three days a month were set aside for emetics and enemas. The Pharaoh had his own Keeper of the Royal Rectum.

Love of enemas outlasted the Pharaoh by thousands of years. Louis XIII, who occupied the French throne from 1610 to 1643, had his insides purged 212 times in one year. Those not lucky enough to be a monarch often had their purges administered by pharmacists who were dubbed *limonadiers du posterior* (lemonade-makers of the ass).

Here comes the enema squad.
Lemonade, anyone?

BOTTOMS UP!

ome will claim that this cure-all actually works—and therefore doesn't belong in this book at all. But most readers, we think, will react to it with a resounding "Yuck!"

It's an elixir that you can drink straight up, mixed with juice or over fruit, steaming hot or chilled. It doesn't cost you a cent and it's readily available to absolutely everybody on the planet.

What is it? Urine, of course.

People have been drinking their pee for religious and medical reasons in different cultures around the globe for thousands of years. Modern-day advocates of urine therapy claim that it's effective against the flu, the common cold, broken bones, toothache, baldness, cancer, dry skin, and just about every other ailment you can think of. Some of them say that information about this anything-but-new-fangled medicine is being suppressed by the medical profession and the drug companies, which don't care for cures from which they cannot profit.

If you want to try it, you might want to talk to your doctor first and have some mouthwash handy.

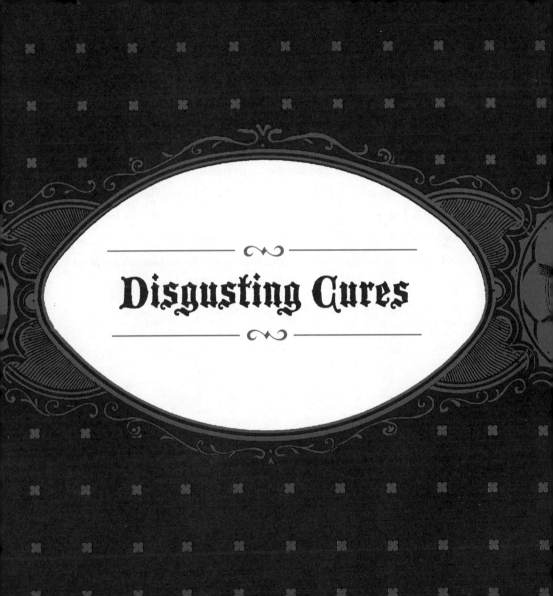

Disgusting Cures

GROSS...AND GROSSER...

If drinking your urine doesn't appeal to you, neither will this advice from the Dictionaire Universelle des Drogues (Universal Dictionary of Drugs), written during the Renaissance by Nicholas Lemery: "Human excrement is a digestive aid, that helps dissolve, soften and ease; it must be used in dried pulverized form and should be swallowed. A single dose should not exceed one dram [a sixteenth of an ounce]."

We'll stick with Pepto-Bismol, thank you.

THIS TOOTH IS KILLING ME!
PASS THE DEAD MOUSE!

G ot a toothache? Try putting a dead mouse on your aching tooth or gum. If you want to be creative, mash the mouse into a paste and mix it with other ingredients of your choosing. This was common practice among ancient Egyptians.

Egyptians weren't the only ones who found dead mice useful. The English in Elizabethan times would split one in half and apply it to a wart to remove it. They also ate them fried or baked in a mouse pie as a cure for bed-wetting. Cooked mice have also been recommended for smallpox, whooping cough, and measles.

THE FART CURE

I f you lived in fourteenth-century Europe, you would have trembled in fear of the Black Death, a disease that struck suddenly and mercilessly, wiping out vast numbers.

Some creative souls believed that foul smells could combat the deadly vapors that were thought to cause the disease. One suggestion was to keep dirty goats in your house. Others used a foul smell accessible to us all: farts. Instead of letting the gas float into the atmosphere, it was suggested, pass it into a jar, then open it when the Black Death was in your neighborhood.

It might also serve to ward off door-to-door salesmen.

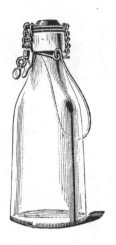

A LOUSY IDEA

aving trouble urinating? Try putting lice in your urinary tract and let them suck out the pee.

This was the proposal of Avicenna of Persia (980–1037) who, this suggestion aside, is considered one of the most brilliant scholars of his day; his *Canon of Medicine* has been called one of the most influential medical textbooks of all time.

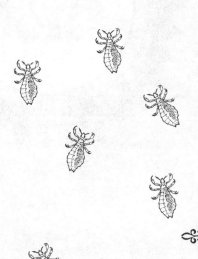

EXTREME
CURES

THANKS, WE'LL JUST MANAGE
WITHOUT THE HAIR

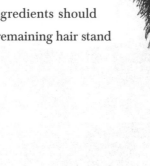

Baldness has always been with us, apparently, and so has the quest for a magic tonic that would make hair sprout on a barren scalp. Around 1550 B.C. an Egyptian medical manual offered this simple formula: Mix together the fats of lion, hippopotamus, crocodile, cat, serpent, and ibex. Douse your bare scalp with it and you'll be hairy once again.

Just gathering the ingredients should be enough to make one's remaining hair stand on end.

FOR ACHING BACKS

S ome medical treatments only *seem* like torture. Here's one that was.

It was called strappado, an orthopedic treatment favored by the ancient Greeks—and a form of torture practiced in medieval times. The patient—or victim—was tied to a ladder, which was then dropped vertically to the ground. The idea was that the displaced vertebrae would be jolted into alignment.

A manuscript from Byzantium around 1100 described the process. Note that the good doctors had thought it out carefully: Patients with curvatures low in the spine were suspended by their feet, while people with curvatures high in the spine got to stay upright. Here's what to do next:

If you're hanging your patient upside down, the doctors advised, lay the ladder on the ground, pad it and tie the patient to it by the ankles. "Then raise the ladder against a high tower or house," the man-

uscript says. "The ground should be solid and the assistants well trained so that they will let the ladder fall smoothly and in a vertical position. . . It is best to drop it from a mast by a pulley." Most alarming is the following: "Jolting is best done with such an apparatus, but it is disagreeable to discuss in detail."

Is your patient right side up? In that case, the doctors advise, "bind the patient firmly to the ladder at his chest, but loosely at his neck, merely enough to keep it straight. Bring his head to the ladder at the forehead. Bind the rest of the body loosely here and there, only to keep it vertical." The legs are allowed to swing freely.

Although Hippocrates, the ancient Greek "father of medicine," disowned the method, strappado was practiced until the nineteenth century. With only slight variation—perhaps the ladder wasn't padded?—it was also used as a means of torture, a practice that reportedly continues to this day.

In strappado, the patient is bound to a ladder and then the ladder is dropped—in an attempt to jolt displaced vertebrae into alignment.

ALTERIVS NON SIT, QVI SVVS ESSE POTEST

AVREOLVS PHILIPPVS THEOPHRASTVS

FORGET THE T.L.C., PASS THE BOILING OIL

oiling oil was routinely poured on wounds during the Renaissance until Paraclesus, a great physician of his day, ran out of it when he was tending to the wounded on a battlefield. He tried a soothing ointment instead and—to his surprise—found that soldiers healed better and suffered less than those treated with hot oil. Medicine became a little less sadistic that day.

 Pictured at left is Paraclesus, one of the more colorful figures of alchemical lore. He was the son of a Swiss doctor and chemist, and was given the name TheophrastusBombastus von Hohenheim at birth, which he later dropped for the more symbolic "Paraclesus."

CURES FOR MENTAL ILLNESS

CRUEL AND UNUSUAL

"Chains, straw, filthy solitude, darkness and starvation; jalap, syrup of buckthorn, tartarised antimony and ipecacuanha administered every spring and fall in fabulous doses to every patient, whether well or ill; spinning in whirligigs, corporal punishment, gagging, continued intoxication; nothing was too wildly extravagant, nothing too monstrously cruel to be prescribed by mad-doctors."

—CHARLES DICKENS

For once, Dickens—who was writing in 1852 of practices that had only recently been abandoned—wasn't guilty of literary license. With no understanding of the causes of mental illness, medicine made the insane fair game for the most experimental therapies. On the next several pages, we describe some of the amazing—and appalling—treatments for the mentally ill that have been tried over the centuries.

THE DROWNING CURE

"Many fools who accidentally fall into water and are dragged out for dead are not only restored to life . . . but also to the full use of their understanding," observed Jan Baptista van Helmont, a Flemish physician practicing in the 1600s. If near-drowning brought sane people to their senses, wouldn't it work for madmen? Dr. van Helmont thought so, and immersed his mentally disturbed patients in water in hopes of extinguishing a "too violent and exorbitant form of fiery life." In the eighteenth century, a Dr. Willard, who ran a private asylum in a small town in New England, tried the same therapy. According to Isaac Ray, a prominent nineteenth-century psychiatrist who co-founded the American Psychiatric Association, "Dr. Willard had a tank prepared on the premises into which the patient, enclosed in a coffin-like box with holes, was lowered. He was kept there until bubbles of air cease to rise, then was taken out, rubbed and revived." The idea was that if the patient was nearly drowned and then brought back to life, "he would take a fresh start, leaving his disease behind."

THE SHAKING CURE

"Shaking out" the madness was one approach to insanity in the 1800s. In London, a physician placed patients in a cage on a pulley and spun them around for a few days. Once the patient was strapped in, the chair would be turned on its axis at top speed, creating a centrifugal force that caused intense pressure to the brain, nausea, and the sensation of suffocation. Not surprisingly, the patient emerged pale, nauseous and, by all reports, less manic. The idea behind this treatment was to reset the patient's equilibrium and brain. That great patriot Dr. Benjamin Rush—known, inexplicably, as "the father of American psychiatry"—liked the shaking cure. He also tried a device known as the "gyrater," which spun the patient around on a board to increase his pulse.

THE SITTING CURE

If shaking didn't work, complete immobility might. Because "madness" was considered an inflammation of the brain, physicians including Dr. Rush liked the "tranquilizer chair." By eliminating all activity, this device was designed to control the flow of blood toward the brain and

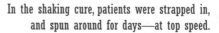

In the shaking cure, patients were strapped in, and spun around for days—at top speed.

lower the pulse. Rush boasted that the chair "binds and confines every part of the body" and "acts as a sedative to the tongue and temper as well as to the blood vessels." The patient's head was locked in a linen-lined wooden box, which blocked his sight. Strong leather bands strapped the patient's chest, arms, and hands to the chair, and pieces of wood held his feet in place. Need a bathroom break? The chair's designers thought of that, too, inserting a "stool-pan" under the chair that could be emptied and replaced as needed. To ensure that absolutely no movement took place, the chair was fastened to the floor. Treatments sometimes went on for six months. It probably felt a lot longer.

THE BLEATING CURE

People who are docile are often described as "lambs." And so it was a logical leap for some doctors in Europe in the 1600s to reason that

transfusing sheep's blood into manic patients "might tame their mad passions." In England in 1667, one purported lunatic was paid twenty shillings to undergo an intravenous transfusion, receiving up to twelve ounces of sheep's blood. (This was medical progress, of sorts; previously patients simply *drank* the blood.) "Some think it may have a good effect upon him as a frantic man by cooling his blood," wrote famed diarist

Samuel Pepys. Following the transfusion, Pepys noted that the patient was "a little cracked in his head, though he speaks very reasonably."

But ovine therapy fell out of favor after a French physician named Jean Denis lost a patient after a transfusion. Bet that doctor felt sheepish.

THE FULL REMOVAL CURE

Less than one hundred years ago, some physicians still believed that mental illness was caused by infected body parts—and that the surgical removal of those body parts could make people sane. "The insane are physically ill," declared Henry Cotton, an American doctor. From an

initial site of infection, he reasoned, bacteria could spread through the lymph or circulatory systems to the brain, where it "finally causes the death of the patient or, if not that, a condition worse than death—a life of mental darkness." Before he retired in 1930, Dr. Cotton ordered 11,000 teeth removed from his patients at Trenton State Hospital in New Jersey. If tooth-pulling didn't cure lunacy, the doctor surgically removed stomachs, gallbladders, colons, testicles, and ovaries. About a third of his patients died. Then Cotton himself went mad (although, given the way he practiced medicine, it could be argued that he already was) and pulled out several of his own teeth. He pronounced himself cured, although he probably only mumbled it.

 In the 1600s, some European doctors believed that transfusing sheep's blood into manic patients would make them as docile as the proverbial lamb.

AN ICE PICK IN THE BRAIN

Medical science made greater progress in the twentieth century than at any other time in history. Yet it was during this period that one incredibly brutal surgery—the lobotomy—became an accepted medical procedure for troublesome patients like schizophrenics.

In a lobotomy, the surgeon usually severs nerve connections to the brain's frontal lobes, which are the seat of emotion and abstract reasoning. As a result, the patient becomes strangely passive—almost robotic.

Between 1936 and the late 1950s, some 50,000 Americans had lobotomies. Many of them were performed by Walter Freeman, a psychiatrist who liked the procedure for everything from neurosis and depression to psychosis and criminality.

So many brains, so little time? Freeman whizzed through the operating room with an ordinary ice pick, sticking it through the thin bone above his patients' eyes with only a local anesthetic. A light tap with a mallet, a brisk turn to the right and left, and a patient who was almost

out of his mind became, well, truly mindless. Freeman perfected an assembly-line approach, whizzing from one patient to the next with his gold-plated ice pick while his assistants timed him to see if he could break his record. Even veteran surgeons fainted at the sight, according to C. George Boeree, a professor who has written about the procedure.

Among Freeman's patients was Rosemary Kennedy, a sister of John F. Kennedy. Mildly retarded from birth, Rosemary was lobotomized at the age of 23 when, biographers say, she began to show interest in men and her father was afraid she would disgrace her family. After her lobotomy she was institutionalized for the rest of her life.

But the procedure's most famous victim is probably the fictitious Randle McMurphy, the rambunctious hero of Ken Kesey's novel *One Flew Over the Cuckoo's Nest*, which was made into a movie starring Jack Nicholson. After leading a rebellion in the psych ward, McMurphy is lobotomized as an act of vengeance. His friend, "the Chief," can't stand to see him so devoid of life and spirit, and smothers him with a pillow.

Royal Cures

THAT MAGIC TOUCH

S crofula, a form of tuberculosis affecting the lymph nodes, was called the "king's evil" during the Enlightenment. What better way to cure it than with the aid of a king? It was widely held in Europe that the "divine right" of kings gave them the power to cure the disease named after them merely by touching the sufferer.

Many subjects waited in line to be cured with a royal touch. Among the last of these in England was the infant Samuel Johnson, who was touched by the last Stuart, Queen Anne. Louis XV of France benevolently took time off during his coronation in 1722 to touch more than 2,000 scrofula victims. The last reported "healing" of this kind was by France's Charles X in 1825.

(Monarchs weren't the only ones whose touch it was believed would cure: Touching an executed man's hand was also recommended, as was touching the rope that hanged him.)

A monarch, exercising his "divine right" to cure disease merely by touching the sufferer.

ROYAL BLOOD

"**N**othing was left untried," said one of the dozen physicians who attended England's Charles II on his deathbed.

He wasn't kidding. After Charles suffered a stroke in 1685 at the age of 55, he was subjected to what can only be described as overkill. With medical care like that, he may well have envied his father, Charles I, who had merely been beheaded.

First, "sixteen ounces of blood were removed from a vein in his right arm with immediate good effect," according to Sir Raymond Crawfurd, a prominent British doctor writing some 300 years later. "As was the approved practice at this time, the king was allowed to remain in the chair in which the convulsions seized him. His teeth were held forcibly open to prevent him biting his tongue." The approach, as a contemporary of the king described it, was to "first to get him to wake, and then to keep him from sleeping."

And, above all, to wring him dry. The doctors applied cupping glasses to the king's shoulders, then dug into him to draw another eight

ounces of blood. They administered something to make him vomit but "as the king could be got to swallow only a small portion of it, they determined to render assistance doubly sure by a full dose of sulphate of zinc"—a chemical later used in electric batteries.

Strong purgatives were given, and supplemented by a succession of clysters, or enemas. "The hair was shorn close, and pungent blistering agents were applied all over his head," Sir Raymond wrote. "And as though this were not enough, the red-hot cautery"—a surgical instrument, usually made of iron—"was requisitioned as well."

The king apologized for being "an unconscionable time a-dying." When he finally did check out, four days into his treatment, it's likely that nobody was more relieved than he was.

'FAMILY' MEDICINE

DO BABY'S TEETH HURT?
HERE, SWEETIE, TAKE SOME OPIUM...

Many nineteenth-century over-the-counter medicines carried the imprimatur of legitimate doctors' names, but contained substances that the FDA nowadays wouldn't dream of permitting without tight control. What's worse, some of these cure-alls were specifically for young children.

Below, a list of some of the patent medicines that no sane individuals would casually imbibe nowadays, much less give their kids:

- **DR. DRAKE'S GERMAN CROUP REMEDY.** Contained opium.
- **DR. JAMES SOOTHING SYRUP.** Contained heroin.
- **DR. SETH ARNOLD'S COUGH KILLER.** Contained morphine.
- **DR. MOFFETT'S TEETHINA AND TEETHING POWDERS.** Contained opium.
- **DR. FAHRNEY'S TEETHING SYRUP.** Contained morphine.
- **GOWAN'S PNEUMONIA CURE.** Contained opium.

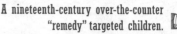

A nineteenth-century over-the-counter "remedy" targeted children.

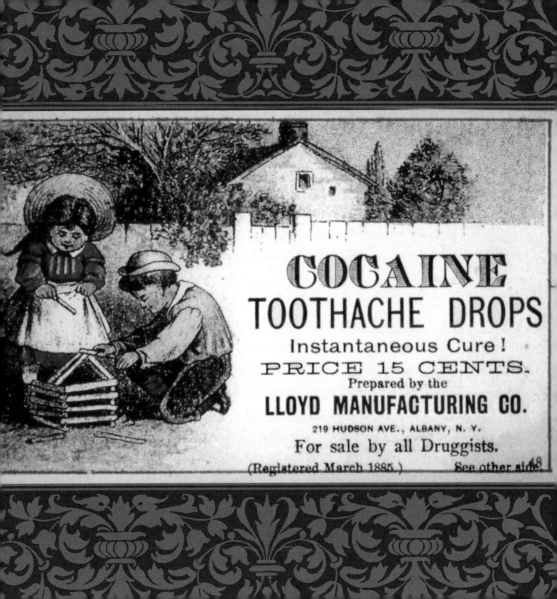

* **ONE DAY COUGH CURE**. Contained cannabis (marijuana) and morphine.
* **PIERCE'S SMART WEED**. Contained opium. (The name of the product was appropriate, except for the word "smart.")
  AND THE LIST GOES ON AND ON.

In 1906, the Pure Food and Drug Act outlawed such over-the-counter tonics—happily for those of us to follow.

To be sure, some patent medicines were harmless, if ineffective. One of them from the 1830s, Dr. Miles Compound Extract of Tomato, was reputed to cure anything from baldness to athlete's foot. It did no such thing, of course, but it tasted good. So good that it's still popular under its modern name: ketchup.

EGG-FREE RECIPES

"Nothing resulted from [doctors'] practice but killing and laming."

Radical words indeed, particularly from a physician. But Paraclesus, a sixteenth-century professor of medicine in the Swiss city of Basel who publicly burned medical tomes whose advice he found spurious, vowed to "abandon such a miserable art and seek truth elsewhere." He sought out cures from common folk, mystics, and occultists and though he is credited with original, often inspired, thinking, his conclusions were often sorely lacking in practicality.

Take, for example, his "recipe" for reproducing human life without the need for a female:

Let the sperm of a man by itself be putrefied in a gourd glass, sealed up, with the highest degree of putrefaction in horse-dung, for the space of forty days or so long until it begin to be

alive, move, and stir, which may easily be seen. After this time it will be something like a man, yet transparent, and without a body. Now after this, if it be every day warily, and prudently nourished and fed with the secret of man's blood, and be for the space of forty weeks kept in a constant, equal heat of horse-dung, it will become a true, and living infant, having all the members of an infant, which is born of a woman, but it will be far less. This we call *Homunculus* or artificial man. . . Now this is one of the greatest secrets, that God ever made known to mortal, sinful man.

It may not have produced a baby. But it's a great way to grow mushrooms.

PUPPY LOVE

Some expectant mothers worry that they'll have difficulty nursing their newborns. For help, look to man's best friend, advised Dr. William Dewees in his *Treatise on the Physical and Medical Treatment of Children*, America's first pediatric guide, published in 1825.

Starting in the eighth month, Dewees declared, a pregnant woman should suckle "a young but sufficiently strong puppy" to toughen and accentuate the nipples, improve secretion, and prevent inflammation. Nursing a puppy, Dewees said, will prepare "the nipples for the future assaults of the child."

Dr. Dewees also had a suggestion for women whose nipples were sunken or short: take a long-stemmed tobacco pipe, plant the bowl on the aureole, and suck it.

A later edition of Dr. Dewees's manual had a suggestion for those who were squeamish about sharing their milk with a member of another species. He observed that a nurse—or any other human—could suck a nipple just as well as a puppy.

ABSTINENCE NEVER LOOKED BETTER

Modern birth control isn't perfect, but it's more reliable—and less repulsive—than it once was. Ancient Egyptian women were advised to coat their cervixes with crocodile dung to prevent unwanted pregnancy. Indian women were advised to use elephant dung.

Say what you will, this method would probably be effective in modern America. What woman would feel like making love after applying such stuff? And what man would want to go near her?

A BOY FOR YOU, A GIRL FOR ME...

Followers of Hippocrates believed that the gender of babies was determined by which of the father's testicles produced the sperm: the right was said to produce males and the left females. Want a girl? Bind the right testicle.

This method may not have guaranteed the desired gender in a baby, but it certainly guaranteed a rather painful experience for the dad in trying.

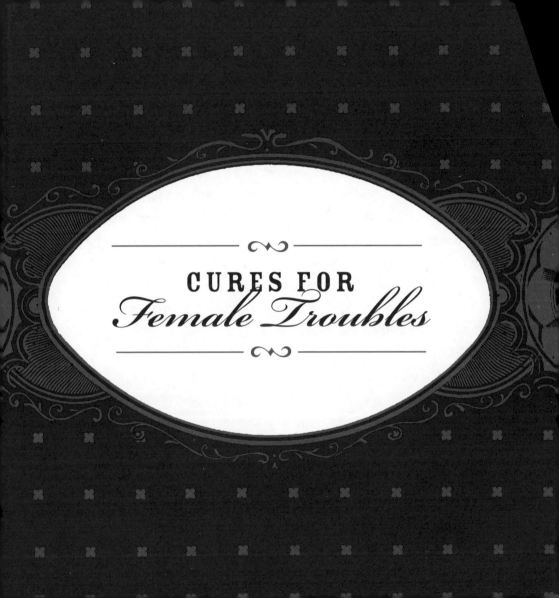

CURES FOR
Female Troubles

DON'T MOVE A MUSCLE

Bed rest is often prescribed for medical problems. But few physicians were as committed to it as Silas Weir Mitchell, an American neurologist who elevated sloth to a fine medical art.

In the late 1800s Mitchell observed that the young women he treated for hysteria were often thin and anemic. His cure was complete bed rest for at least six weeks.

"At first, and in some cases for four or five weeks, I do not permit the patient to sit up or to sew or write or read," he wrote in his book, invitingly titled *Fat and Blood*.

The only action allowed is that needed to clean the teeth. In some instances I have not permitted the patient to turn over without aid, and this I have done because sometimes I think no motion desirable, and because sometimes the moral influence of absolute repose is of use. In such cases I arrange to have the bowels and water passed while lying down, and the patient is

lifted on to a lounge at bedtime and sponged, and then lifted back again into the newly-made bed.

The patient drank milk, and lots of it. She was fed by a nurse when she progressed to solid food, and later her meat was cut up so she could feed herself more easily. Putting away several substantial meals a day, she was expected to gain as much as fifty pounds. The rest cure also involved massage and electrical stimulation, so the patient's muscles didn't completely atrophy.

Among upper-class American women, Mitchell's rest cure became all the rage. He wrote,

I am daily amazed to see how kindly nervous and anemic women take to this absolute rest, and how little they complain of its monotony. From a restless life of irregular hours, and probably endless drugging, from hurtful sympathy and over-zealous care, the patient passes to an atmosphere of quiet, to order and control, to the system and care of a thorough nurse,

to an absence of drugs, and to simple diet. The result is always at first, whatever it may be afterwards, a sense of relief, and a remarkable and often a quite abrupt disappearance of many of the nervous symptoms with which we are all of us only too sadly familiar.

But not everybody was so keen on the rest cure. One of his patients, Charlotte Perkins Gilman, wrote a short story, "The Yellow Wallpaper," about a woman who, like herself, suffered from postpartum depression. In the story, the narrator worries that her husband will be displeased by her slow convalescence. "If I don't pick up faster," she frets, "he shall send me to Weir Mitchell in the fall."

SHE'S GOTTA HAVE IT

A woman interested in sex? Off with her clitoris!

At the height of Victorian prudishness, a woman who displayed any interest in sex was considered a nymphomaniac—and certifiably insane. According to historian Ann Goldberg, a woman could be locked up for nymphomania if she was promiscuous, bore illegitimate children, was a victim of sexual assault or rape, was caught masturbating, or merely exhibited "man-craziness"—an expression used back then to describe flirting.

When a woman was brought to the asylum, a doctor gave her a pelvic exam. If her clitoris looked supersized, she was institutionalized on the spot. She would be pronounced cured and released only if the clitoris returned to a more, dare we say, feminine size.

Treatments for nymphomania included separation from men, bloodletting, induced vomiting, cold douches over the head, warm douches over the breasts, leeches applied to the vulva, solitary confinement, straitjackets, and a bland diet. And, of course, there was the

clitoridectomy, also known as "extirpation"—pulling it out by the roots.

The chief advocate of clitoridectomies was Isaac Baker Brown, a London gynecologist surgeon in the 1800s. In his view, masturbation (or "excessive venereal indulgence") could lead to hysteria, followed by

spinal irritation, hysterical epilepsy, cataleptic fits, epileptic fits, idiocy, mania, and finally, death.

Baker Brown's cure? Cut out the clitoris with scissors, pack the wound with lint, and administer opium via the rectum. Within a month, the woman would be on her way to becoming a "happy and healthy wife and mother," Baker Brown wrote. He added, "If medical and surgical treatment were brought to bear, all such unhappy measures such as divorce would be obviated."

In 1867, however, he was expelled from the Obstetrical Society of London. It wasn't that other doctors didn't perform clitoridectomies; rather, they resented the way he hogged the spotlight for the same procedure they carried out quietly. He was criticized, too, for operating without informed consent—of the husbands!

GOOD VIBRATIONS

If an apple a day keeps the doctor away, plenty of women must have shunned apples during the Victorian era. That's because some women enjoyed their only orgasms at the hands of their friendly practitioner.

How did doctors become responsible for dispensing orgasms? Since at least Hippocrates, it was believed that hysteria was a uniquely feminine malady, caused by the irregular movement of blood from the uterus to the brain; the word *hysteria* comes from the Greek for uterus, *hystera*. It explained why women were sometimes irritable, depressed, weepy, even ticklish. Traditional intercourse provided little relief, and masturbation was frowned upon. "In effect," historian Rachel Maines says in her book, *The Technology of Orgasm: "Hysteria," the Vibrator, and Women's Sexual Satisfaction*, "doctors inherited the task of producing orgasm in women because it was a job nobody else wanted."

And so began the medical practice of regular "vulvalar" massage. The 1899 edition of the *Merck Manual*, a reference guide for physicians,

lists massage as a treatment for hysteria (along with treating nymphomania with sulfuric acid). And in a 1903 commentary on treatments for hysterical patients, Samuel Howard Monell wrote that "pelvic massage (in gynecology) has its brilliant advocates and they report wonderful results."

"I'm sure the women felt much better afterward, slept better, smiled more," Maines says. Besides, she adds, hysteria was traditionally defined as an incurable, chronic disease—and a lucrative one: "The patient had to go to the doctor regularly. She didn't die. She was a cash cow."

Still, it was slow work for the doctors. "Most of them did it because they felt it was their duty," comments Maines. "It wasn't sexual at all." That's why they welcomed the introduction of the electromechanical vibrator in the early 1880s. The vibrator reduced a time-consuming, labor-intensive task to a matter of minutes or even seconds. A text from 1883 called *Health For Women* recommended the new vibrators for treating pelvic hyperemia, or congestion of the genitalia. (Water sprays also enjoyed some popularity.)

By the turn of the century, at least two dozen models were available to the medical profession. There were musical vibrators, counter-

weighted vibrators, vibratory forks, undulating wire coils called vibratiles, vibrators that hung from the ceiling, vibrators attached to tables, floor models on rollers, and portable devices that fit in the palm of the hand. They were powered by electric current, battery, foot pedal, water turbine, gas engine, or air pressure, and they vibrated at frequencies of 1,000 to 7,000 pulses per minute. Prices ranged from a low of $15 to what Maines calls the "Cadillac of vibrators," an elaborate device that cost $200 plus freight charges in 1904.

But within a couple of decades women, hysterical and otherwise, were taking matters into their own hands. They ordered their own vibrators—along with their sewing machines and toasters—from Sears, Roebuck catalogs. No prescription required.

During the Victorian era, some women enjoyed their only orgasms at the hands of their doctors.

IRREPRODUCIBLE RESULTS

Ovaries. Who needs 'em?

Not women, seemed to be the answer of Robert Battey, a respected American surgeon operating in the second half of the 1800s. After successfully removing an enormous ovarian cyst, Battey came to believe that even healthy ovaries should be removed to relieve symptoms ranging from menstrual pain to neurosis and insanity.

Battey stated his views in his 1873 book, *Female Castration*. (From the title, you might think he condemned the practice. You'd be wrong.)

The operation Battey popularized, the curiously named "normal ovariotomy," was performed into the twentieth century. The subjects typically were young women diagnosed with "ovariomania"—a psychological disorder affecting women of childbearing age. Many of them died in surgery. Survivors, of course, abandoned any thoughts of motherhood.

Still, Battey wasn't the only, well, batty physician when it came to treating women's "problems." His contemporary, a feminist doctor named Alice B. Stockham, believed that all female complaints were psychological. The mind, she said, could control even malignant tumors.

CURES

FOR

MALE TROUBLES

RX FOR SELF-ABUSE: MEDICAL ABUSE

The Victorians held very strong opinions about masturbation by boys and men. They considered it a vile habit that could lead to acne, epilepsy, mental retardation, blindness, and death—in other words, just about everything undesirable. Here are some ways that were suggested to curb a young man's efforts to self-indulge.

* Hand restraints. The boy's wrists would be tied to the bedpost at night, or he would be put to bed in straitjacket pajamas.
* Fastening the foreskin with rings, clasps or staples. If the boy wasn't circumcised, he might have his foreskin sewn up—allowing, of course, a sufficient opening for urination.
* Eating healthy foods. Both Sylvester Graham, inventor of the Graham cracker, and John Harvey Kellogg, developer of corn flakes, suggested that their products would decrease a lad's evil impulses.
* Electric erection alarms. A flexible metal band, attached by

wires to an **alarm**, was wrapped around the base of the penis at night. The alarm would notify parents when their boy was "abusing" himself or was about to suffer a nocturnal emission, which was considered equally unhealthy.

❋   Last but not least: Ice water enemas.

A chastity belt to presumably protect
young men from themselves.

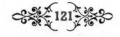

HARD-WIRED FOR LOVE

Was there anything electricity *couldn't* fix? Not in the view of Julius Althaus, a Victorian surgeon who recommended applying electric current to cure impotence. Stick an electrode up the penis, Althaus advised, place another electrode on the lower back, and run a current between the two. Bzzzt! The blockages are cleared out, and a new man rises from the operating table.

But things could get sticky: The electrode tended to become fused to the mucous membrane inside the penis. Left unattended, the patient would never again have a problem getting rigid. To free the flesh and remove the electrode, the doctor had to reverse the current. "If skillfully performed," Althaus wrote, "this somewhat complicated proceeding is not unpleasant."

Maybe not. But it sure helps explain why Viagra caught on.

A DOCTOR WITH BALLS

Ever since Pan, the nymph-chasing cloven-hoofed Greek god, goats have been equated with lechery. So it was not unreasonable for a Kansas doctor in the 1920s to assert that he could cure male impotence by transplanting a bit of goat testicle into his patients' scrotums.

Become "the-ram-that-am-with-every-lamb," urged Dr. John R. Brinkley, and thousands of men flocked to his clinic in the small town of Milford. According to one report, the goateed (!) doctor even let his patients choose from the herd in his own backyard. His burgeoning business led to this joke:

Q: What's the fastest thing on four legs?
A: A goat passing Dr. Brinkley's hospital.

Some patients swore that they were able to father children after the procedure, and for a time the American Medical Association left him

alone. What brought the doctor down was overzealous marketing. On his radio station, which he'd built to entertain the patients who came to his clinic, Brinkley offered prescriptions by mail. In 1929 the newly formed Federal Communications Commission took away his license.

For a time he broadcast from Mexico, according to *Border Radio*, a book by Gene Fowler and Bill Crawford. But in 1939 the U.S. persuaded Mexico to shut down that station, too, and Dr. Brinkley—quite ma-a-a-d to the end—died in 1942.

IT PAYS TO RECONSIDER...

Every once in a while, a treatment rejected by the medical establishment gains respectability. Chiropractory, once dismissed as nonsense by physicians, is now licensed and covered by insurance. Acupuncture, too, has gained respect in the U.S. Pharmaceutical companies have appropriated ancient folk remedies.

The most dramatic return to favor, however, involves a humble worm: the leech.

Most people would share Humphrey Bogart's crazed reaction to the little bloodsuckers when they assaulted him in the swamp in *The African Queen*. But it turns out that, medically speaking, leeches have many virtues.

Modern researchers have discovered that leeches' saliva contains natural anticoagulants, as well as substances that liquefy hardening blood and open blood vessels to increase blood flow, according to a recent *New Yorker* article by John Colapinto. In other words, leech spit turns out to be a miracle drug.

And leech saliva contains a natural anesthetic that minimizes the pain you might expect from being bitten by their three hundred mini sawing teeth, arranged in three jaws.

Doctors have found leeches to be useful in restoring circulation following microsurgical operations, such as the reattachment of fingers and ears. The FDA has given its stamp of approval, the second time it has authorized the use of a live animal. (The first was for the use of maggots, which are applied to wounds to consume infected tissue.)

What does this tell us? Maybe: Keep your mind open—not only to new ideas but to old ones as well.

PICTURE CREDITS

p. 11: Quack, woodcut illustration, 17th century, from the Roxburghe Ballads, volume 4, part 2, page 358. Mary Evans Picture Library.

p. 16: Adverse effects of mercury treatment, color lithograph by James Morison, published in London, ca. 1850. Wellcome Library, London.

p. 24: *Breathing a Vein*, etching by James Gillray, published London by H. Humphrey, Jan. 28, 1804. National Library of Medicine, Bethesda, MD.

p. 36: *Le Baquet de Mesmer*, detail engraving, ca. late 1770s. Wellcome Library, London.

p. 39: *Metallic-Tractors*, etching by James Gillray, published in London by H. Humphrey, Nov. 11, 1801. National Library of Medicine, Bethesda, MD.

p. 45: Adrian Shoe Fluoroscope, photograph, ca. 1930. Otis Historical Archives, AFIP. National Library of Medicine, Bethesda, MD.

p. 48: Woman applying a leech to forearm, wood engraving by Guillaume van den Bossche, published in Brussels by Joannis Mommarti, 1639. National Library of Medicine, Bethesda, MD.

p. 49: *De La Lancette*, bloodletting instruments, engraving, author Jean Jacques Perret, published in Paris, 1771-72. National Library of Medicine, Bethesda, MD.

pp. 50–51: A man reading with the aid of spectacles (left), and surgical procedure for cataract, wood engraving book illustrations from <u>Ophthalmodouleia, das ist, Augendienst</u> by Georg Batisch, published Dreszden (Dresden), 1583. National Library of Medicine, Bethesda, MD.

p. 54: Palate and tongue surgery in nine vignettes, published in <u>Armamentarium chirurgicum bipartitum</u> by Johannes Francofurti Scultetus, 1666. National Library of Medicine, Bethesda, MD.

p. 59: A skull being trepanned, detail, engraving with etching by B.L. Prevost after Louis-Jacques Goussier, ca. late 1700s. Wellcome Library, London.

p. 62: *Apothicaire. Servez la bavaroise.* by Charles Philipon, detail, lithograph, published France, ca. 1850s. National Library of Medicine, Bethesda, MD.

p. 75: Strappado or Greek ladder treatment, detail, published in <u>Apollonius Citiensis,</u> Leipzig, 1896. Wellcome Library, London.

p. 76: Portrait of Paraclesus. National Library of Medicine, Bethesda, MD.

p. 83: Illustration of whirling chair, detail, published in <u>Traité sur l'alienation mentale et sur les hospices des alienes</u> by Joseph Guislain, Amsterdam, 1826. National Library of Medicine, Bethesda, MD.

p. 86: Blood transfusion from a lamb, detail, engraving published in <u>Armamentarii Chirurgici</u> by Johannes Schultes (1595-1645), Amsterdam, 1672. Bibliotheque de la Faculte de Medecine, Paris, France, Archives Charmet/ Bridgeman Art Library.

p. 93: le Royte teuche (Royal Touch), book illustration published in Therapeutique Magnetique, by Baron Du Potet, Paris, 1863. Mary Evans Picture Library.

p. 99: Cocaine Toothache Drops, trade card, 1895. National Library of Medicine, Bethesda, MD.

p. 116: Photograph of a young woman using a *Sanofix* electric vibrator from a printed advertisement. Berlin, 1913. Wellcome Library, London.